A Panoramic View From Bunker Hill Monument

James Smillie

In the interest of creating a more extensive selection of rare historical book reprints, we have chosen to reproduce this title even though it may possibly have occasional imperfections such as missing and blurred pages, missing text, poor pictures, markings, dark backgrounds and other reproduction issues beyond our control. Because this work is culturally important, we have made it available as a part of our commitment to protecting, preserving and promoting the world's literature. Thank you for your understanding.

A PANORAMIC VIEW FROM BUNKER HILL MONUMENT.

ENGRAVED BY JAMES SMILLIE,

FROM A

DRAWING BY R. P. MALLORY.

BOSTON:
REDDING & CO. 8 STATE STREET,
*And for sale by H. Long & Brother; W. H. Graham; Burgess, Stringer & Co.,
New York; and Zeiber & Co., Philadelphia.*
1848.

Price 75 cents.

WHITE & POTTER, Printers, Spring Lane, Boston.

PERSPECTIVE VIEW OF BUNKER HILL MONUMENT.

PANORAMIC VIEW

FROM

BUNKER HILL MONUMENT

THE view from Bunker Hill Monument, for varied beauty and extent, is one of the finest in the world — and is rendered doubly interesting from the fact of its embracing so many places intimately associated with important events connected with the history and patriotism of the country.

This engraving, and explanatory key, are published to meet a want long felt by strangers visiting the monument, and who are unacquainted with the localities in the neighborhood. It is hoped, however, from the very careful and faithful manner in which the work has been accomplished, that it will meet a welcome reception from the residents of the cities and towns included in the landscape.

The city of Boston, and its relation to the surrounding country, is very favorably presented to the eye from this point of view. At one glance is seen all the railroads — seven in number — and every other avenue connecting Boston with the country — excepting, only, the two bridges from South Boston, and Washington street, over the neck. The position of these last named places, however, cannot fail to be understood.

The commerce and trade of Boston are increasing with an unparalleled rapidity — mainly attributable to her railroads. There are now — May, 1848 — *two hundred and twenty-eight trains of cars* passing over the railroads in Boston *every day*. In 1845, these roads carried *two millions two hundred and fifty-four thousand six hundred and eighty passengers* to and from Boston. Last year — 1847 — these same roads carried *four millions seventy-five thousand six hundred and ninety-eight passengers*, nearly doubling their number in three years. The number of passengers and tons of freight carried over each road in 1847, will be found in the key, under the figure designating the road.

With the accompanying key will be found some little historical and statistical matter, interesting to those with whom it is not already familiar; also a very brief notice of the Battle of Bunker Hill, and an account of the Monument.

A KEY TO THE ENGRAVING.

1. *Eastern Railroad.* — Capital stock $2,520,000. This road was opened in 1838, and with its branches and connections, now extends about 125 miles. Its extreme eastern terminus is in Portland, Me. In 1847 there were 892,896 passengers carried over this road, and 41,047 tons of freight. Twenty-four trains of cars pass over this road daily. Depot on Eastern avenue, Commercial street, Boston, and at East Boston.

1½. *Chelsea Creek Bridge.* — A bridge across Chelsea Creek, connecting East Boston with Chelsea.

2. *Butler's Iron Foundry,* East Boston.

3. *United States Navy Yard.* — The walls of this yard enclose about 60 acres of ground. The dry dock, in the yard, is 341 feet in length, 80 in width, and 30 feet deep. "Old Ironsides" was the first vessel floated within its walls for repairs. Visitors are freely permitted to visit the yard every day, except Sunday, and receive polite and kind attention.

4. Four or five dwelling-houses belonging to the navy yard, for the residence of officers on duty there.

4½. *Glindon Iron Works.*

5. *Timber Sheds.* — These large buildings, called timber sheds, are 450 feet in length, and are used for seasoning the lumber used in the construction of U. S. vessels.

6. *Rope-Walk.* — This is one of the best rope-walks in the world, and supplies the United States government with all its cordage. It is 1350 feet in length. The machinery is driven by a very large and beautiful steam engine. It is well worth visiting.

7. *Graves Island.* — The most distant island in Boston harbor. Good fishing-ground near it.

8. *Green Islands.* — A group of islands on the margin of the "*Broad Sound.*"

9. *Point Shirley* is the southernmost part of Chelsea. The space between Point Shirley and Deer Island, which is opposite, is called "Shirley Gut." The smelting works of the Revere Copper Co. are on this point.

10. *Deer Island.* — The space between Deer Island and Long Island is called "The Broad Sound."

11. *Apple Island* is a very pleasant island between Point Shirley and East Boston.

12. *Pulling Point* is about half way between East Boston and Point Shirley.

13. *East Boston,* (*formerly Noddle's Island.*) — This island is about 1800 feet from Boston. It was purchased in 1832 by a company of gentlemen, and the first house built there was in the month of October of that year. It contains several large manufacturing establishments, and a large sugar refinery, celebrated for the quantity and quality of its sugar. Ferry-boats ply between East Boston and the city every five minutes. East Boston and all the islands in Boston harbor belong to ward four of the city of Boston.

14. *East Boston Steam Flour Mill.*
15. *Sugar House.* — East Boston.
15½. *East Boston Iron and Gas Company*
16. United States line-of-battle ship *Franklin*, of 74 guns.
17. *Ship Houses.* — In these houses are built the ships for the United States service.
18. *Machine shop*, and blacksmith shop, belonging to the United States.
19. *Quay wall*, and battery.
20. *Timber Dock.* — This dock is constantly filled with timber, which is soaked here in the salt water for months, and sometimes for years, before being used in the construction of ships.
21. *Naval Store Houses.* — In these large and commodious buildings are kept the various articles belonging to the ships of the navy, such as sails, rigging, hammocks, &c., &c.
22. *Steam Engine House, and Work Shop.* — The steam engine in this building is used principally for emptying the dry dock after a vessel has been floated in. Gun carriages are made in this building.
23. *Commodore's House.* — This house is in the navy yard, and is occupied by the commandant of the yard. It is familiarly known as " *The Commodore's House.*"
24. *Ohio*, 74. — Full-rigged, and at anchor off the navy yard.
25. *Jamestown sloop-of-war.* — When this drawing was made, the Jamestown lay where she is here represented, landing her guns, and being fitted out for her mission of charity to Ireland.
26. *Bomb Ketch Stromboli*, in the dry dock, previous to her departure for Vera Cruz.
27. *Officers' Houses.* — This block of houses is occupied by officers belonging to the navy yard.
28. *Great Calf Island, and Great and Middle Brewster.* — From Bunker Hill Monument these islands seem like one. The land to the right is the Great Brewster — that to the left is Great Calf Island. The Middle Brewster is hid from view behind Great Calf Island.
29. *Outer Brewster.* — Good fishing ground near this island.
30. *Boston Light* is a short distance south-east of Great Brewster.
31. *Point Alderton* is the extreme northern point of Nantasket Beach.
32. *George's Island*, (*Fort Warren.*) — This island has recently been *very strongly* fortified, and is well worth visiting.
33. *Lovel's Island.* — The space between Lovel's Island and Deer Island is the " Broad Sound."
34. *Nix's Mate.* — A very small shoal with a monument on it to mark its locality.
35. *Gallop Island* lies between Nix's Mate and George's Island.
36. *Long Island, and Long Island Light.* — There is also a marine telegraphic station on this island, near the light house.
37. *Governor's Island*, (*Fort Winthrop.*) — This island is fortified — is opposite Boston on the east, and north of Fort Independence about three fourths of a mile. Governor's Island and Castle Island separate the inner from the outer harbor.

38. *Cunard Steamers' Landing*, at East Boston. — A fine wharf, 1000 feet long, was built for the accommodation of these steamers, and the free use of it given them for 20 years.

39. *East Boston Ferry Boat.* — These are substantial and commodious steamboats. They leave each end of the ferry every five minutes, during the day and evening.

40. *Chelsea Ferry Boat.* — These are well built and commodious steamers, and ply between Chelsea and Boston from daylight till eleven o'clock at night.

41. *Cohasset* is about 20 miles from Boston. Incorporated 1770. A favorite resort during the summer months. Beautiful maritime scenery — a long and elegant beach — good fishing and fine sea air are always to be found there.

42. *Hull* is situated very pleasantly on the peninsula of *Nantasket*, about nine miles from Boston. Incorporated 1644. It has a fine beach, four miles long; plenty of fish, &c., and is much frequented by parties during the hot weather.

43. *Hingham* was settled in 1633. Is fourteen miles from Boston. Built at the head of a fine cove, and is an exceedingly beautiful place. A steamboat leaves Boston three times a day for Hingham. Population about 5000.

44. *Rainsford Island* contains about twelve acres of land, and is about six miles from the city. It has been the only regular quarantine ground since the country was settled. There are several fine houses on it for the sick, and for others who arrive from sea. The health officer resides there, permanently, from the 15th June to the 15th September. Dr. J. V. C. Smith has been the health officer since 1826. All the buildings on the island are white; while the gravel walks, great variety of fruit trees, and highly cultivated gardens, give the quarantine ground a most agreeable and inviting appearance.

45. *Pettick's Island.*

46. *Spectacle Island.* — So named from its resemblance to a pair of spectacles.

47. *Castle Island, (Fort Independence.)* — This island and fort is on the south side of the channel; was formerly used as a place of confinement for criminals.

48. *Pumpkin Island.*

49. *Slate Island.*

50. *Grape Island.*

51. *Weymouth* is about eleven miles from Boston. Indian name Wessagassett. Settled 1624. A very pleasant town. Owns 1000 tons of shipping. Population about 5000.

52. *Sheep Island.*

53. *Quincy.* — First settled 1625, by Captain Wollaston. Incorporated 1792. Quincy has the honor of having given two Presidents to the United States. About nine miles from Boston. Population about 6000.

54. *Nut Island.*

55. *Moon Island.*

56. *Thompson's Island.* — The Boston Asylum and Farm School have located their noble institution on this island. The "Boston Asylum for Indigent Boys" was incorporated in 1814. In 1835 the boys were removed from the city to Thompson's Island. Subsequently the "Farm School" was united with it, and the island purchased from money subscribed for the purpose. There are 140 acres of land on the island. The object of this institution is to rescue from poverty and neglect, from temptation and vice, those who have been left without parents or without friends. It is one of the noblest and most useful charities in the land.

57. *Dorchester* (or South Boston) *Point*.

58. *South Boston* was formerly a part of Dorchester, and contains about 600 acres of land. It was separated from Dorchester and united to Boston, in 1804. In 1800 there was but one house on the lot.

59. *City Buildings.* — These buildings are on land owned by the city, and consist of an Asylum for Lunatics, House of Correction, House of Reformation, House of Industry, Alms House, and Hospital. The city land, in this lot, consists of 100 acres. A portion of it is well cultivated.

60. *Quincy Bay.* — A handsome, broad bay, before the town of Quincy.

61. *Squantum* is the name given to a strip of rough, rocky land, about a mile in length, which projects from the coast between Quincy and Dorchester Bays. Its Indian name was "Mos-we-tu-sett," and some have supposed that from this was derived the name of the state. It is a "great" place for fishing, and chowder, and their concomitants.

62. *The Perkins Institution for the Blind* is located on the summit of Mount Washington, in South Boston. It was incorporated in 1829, under the name of the "New England Institution for the Blind" — but its name was subsequently changed, in consequence of a munificent donation made it by the Hon. T. H. Perkins of Boston. Dr. S. G. Howe has been the superintendent or director of this institution from its infancy to the present time.

63. *Telegraphic Station* on Central Wharf, for announcing the arrival of vessels in the harbor below. The outer telegraphic station is on Nantasket, the next on Long Island, the last two in the city, one on Central Wharf, and one on the old State House.

64. *Old Forts on Dorchester* (*now South Boston*) *Heights.* — These heights completely command the harbor and city of Boston, and were taken possession of and fortified by the Americans in March, 1776, causing the British immediately to evacuate the city of Boston, where they had established their head quarters.

65. *Savin Hill*, in Dorchester, is one of the loveliest places in the vicinity of Boston, and a favorite resort in summer.

66. *Boston Custom House.* — Located at the head of, and between, Central and Long Wharves. A substantial and splendid granite edifice. Ammi B. Young, architect. Building completed in 1847.

67. *Quincy Market.* — Built in 1827. Is 536 feet long, by 50 wide. Built of Quincy granite, at a cost of $150,000, exclusive of the land on which it stands. The street on its north side is 65 feet wide, and that on the south 102 feet. It contains 131 stalls. Its chambers are used for stores and

armories. Called "Quincy" from the name of its founder, the Hon. Josiah Quincy, Mayor of Boston for several years.

68. *Faneuil Hall*, or the old "Cradle of Liberty." — Built 1742, and presented to the town of Boston by Peter Faneuil. Its hall, 76 feet square by 28 high, is ornamented with some good paintings, — two, Washington and Knox, by Gilbert Stuart, and a portrait of Samuel Adams, by Copley.

69. *Merchant's Exchange* is on the south side of State street. The post-office and merchant's reading room are in this building.

70. *Copp's Hill Grave Yard.* — It was on this spot that a heavy battery was planted by the British in 1775, and from which the carcasses were thrown that burned Charlestown.

71. *Gas Works.* — These buildings were erected by the Boston Gas Light Company, for manufacturing gas.

72. *Charlestown Common.* — A pretty spot near the foot of the monument.

73. *Old Colony Railroad.* — Capital stock $1,900,000. This road was opened in November, 1845. It reaches to Plymouth, and with its branches and connections extends over 75 miles. In 1847 there were 389,994 passengers, and 42,707 tons of freight carried over this road. Twenty-eight trains pass over this road daily. Depot corner of Kneeland and South streets.

74. *Dorchester* is about four miles from Boston. Indian name, "Mattapan." Incorporated 1630. A beautiful town with 10 or 12,000 inhabitants, and contains many elegant country seats. Railroad cars and omnibusses pass through it almost every hour.

75. *South Bay.* — The large bay on the east side of Boston neck.

76. *Depot of Fitchburg Railroad.* — A large and handsome granite building at the foot of Haverhill street, not quite finished, but will probably be completed by the 1st of July, 1848. The depot of this road is now in Charlestown, near Warren Bridge.

77. *Charlestown Bridge* was the first bridge built in this country. Completed in 1786. Is now free.

78. *Warren Bridge* was built in 1828, and is also free.

79. *Mansion House Hotel.* — This is a pleasantly situated and commodious hotel, fronting on Charlestown Square.

80. *Charlestown Market House.*

81. *Mount Pleasant, Roxbury.* — A pleasant place; overlooking Boston, the harbor and islands. A favorite place of residence. Omnibusses run here from Boston every fifteen minutes.

82. *Roxbury* joins Boston. Incorporated 1630. Became a city in 1847. Birth place of General Warren. Exceedingly beautiful city, and well worth visiting. Population about 18,000. Omnibusses run constantly between Boston and Roxbury; also Providence, Dedham, and Stoughton railroad cars.

83. *Boston, and State House.* — The State House crowns the city of Boston, and was built near the summit of Beacon Hill, in 1798. In it may be seen a marble statue of Washington, by Chantrey, and many relics of the revolution. Also the halls of the senate and house of representatives, room of the governor and council, and the state library. From the cupola of the State House may be seen the

finest panoramic view in the world. The city of Boston was incorporated in 1630. In 1648 all the inhabitants were accommodated in one church. The population at the present time is about 130,000. Became a city in 1822. Boston consists of three parts, viz.: Old Boston, East Boston, and South Boston. South Boston was part of Dorchester, and was united to Boston in 1804. Boston is the second commercial city in the Union, and fifth in population. Contains about 120 literary and charitable societies, nearly 100 churches, 102 newspapers and magazines, about 800 streets and avenues, and 116 wharves, — many of the latter very long and commodious.

84. *Depot of Maine Railroad* is in Haymarket Square, Boston.

85. *Depot of Lowell Railroad* is in Lowell Street, Boston.

86. *Fitchburgh Railroad.* — Capital stock $2,116,100. This road was opened on the 5th March, 1845. With its branches and connections now extends about 135 miles. In 1848 there were 494,035 passengers, and 244,476 tons of freight carried over this road. Thirty-four trains pass over this road daily. Depot, at present, in Charlestown, near Warren Bridge, but will soon be removed (about first of July, 1848) to the new depot in Haverhill street, Boston.

87. *Maine Railroad.* — Capital stock $2,974,000. This road was opened in 1836. With its branches and connections now extends about 122 miles. In 1848 there were 726,307 passengers, and 120,428 tons of freight carried over this road. Thirty-four trains pass over this road every day. Depot in Haymarket Square.

88. *Lowell Railroad.* — Capital stock $1,800,000. This road opened in June, 1835. With its branches and connections now extends about 160 miles. In 1848 there were 484,683 passengers, and 281,441 tons of freight carried over this road. Twenty-eight trains pass over this road daily. Depot in Lowell street.

89. *Cragie's Bridge* was opened in 1809. Length, 2796 feet. Will become property of the state in 1879.

90. *Cambridge Bridge* was opened November 23, 1793. Length, 2758 feet; abutment and causeway, 3432; whole length, 6190 feet. Becomes state property in 1879.

91. *Mill Dam* was three years being built. Opened July 2, 1821. One and a half miles long, and cost $700,000. On it are some large mills, with powerful machinery, for making railroad iron.

92. *Worcester Railroad.* — Capital stock $3,500,000. This road was opened in 1834. The first train of passenger cars that ever left Boston, went out on this road on the morning of April 1, 1834. With its branches and connections, this road extends about 450 miles, this side of Albany, N. Y. At Albany it connects with other roads, that extend to Lakes Erie and Ontario— making the whole distance of its branches and connections about *seven hundred miles*. In 1848 there were 598,305 passengers, and 283,718 tons of freight carried over this road. Fifty-two trains pass over this road daily. Depot in Beach street.

93. *Providence Railroad.* — Capital stock $2,520,000. This road opened in June, 1834. With its branches and connections it now extends about 135 miles. In 1848 there were 487,478 passengers,

and 87,605 tons of freight carried over this road. Twenty-eight trains pass over this road every day. Depot in Charles street, foot of the common.

94. *Back Bay.* — The waters of this bay and South Bay formerly met over the neck during the spring and fall tides. But the neck has been defended by a dyke, and raised considerably within a few years, so that this avenue to the city is perfectly protected.

95. *Tremont Road.* — This road passes between Roxbury and Boston, over the neck, on the west side of Washington street.

96. *Chimney of the Roxbury Laboratory, in Roxbury.* — This chimney is 202 feet in height.

97. *Brookline,* formerly part of Boston; set off and incorporated in 1705. Distant about six miles. A beautiful place; full of rich, rural scenery, and many fine seats. Population about 2000. Omnibusses run there constantly.

98. *Railroad Car Houses.* — Places of deposit for cars and engines belonging to the railroads.

99. *Cambridgeport.* — A part of Cambridge.

100. *East Cambridge.* — A part of Cambridge. The Cambridge Glass Works are located here, and may be seen from the monument.

101. *Cragie's Point Bridge.* — Extends from Cragie's Bridge to Charlestown.

102. *Brighton,* formerly part of Cambridge. Set off and incorporated 1807. The famous cattle fair is held here every week. It is a beautiful place, with highly cultivated grounds. Population about 2000. Distant about five miles. Omnibusses run there three times a day, and railroad cars almost every hour.

103. *Cambridge Port.* — A part of Cambridge.

104. *East Cambridge.* — [See 100.]

105. *State Prison.* — This building is distinctly seen from the monument, on the west side of Charlestown. Its walls enclose about five acres. Visitors are admitted any day in the week, by paying 25 cents. There are generally between 250 and 300 convicts confined here.

106. *Charles River.* — The mouth of Charles River which empties into Boston Harbor, between Charlestown and Boston, helps to make these two peninsulas. This river is about 50 miles in length, and navigable for a considerable distance from its mouth.

107. *Cambridge* is four miles distant. Settled in 1631. First called Newton. Became a city in 1847. The first college in this country was commenced there in 1636. In 1638 Rev. John Harvard gave about $4000 towards its endowment. At this time the name of the town was changed to Cambridge. The college library contains about 50,000 volumes. The college is called Harvard, after its founder. Its minerals, philosophical apparatus, anatomical museum, chemicals, botanic garden, &c., &c., are extensive and valuable. Cambridge is a beautiful town, and should be visited. Washington's head quarters were in Cambridge, and may still be seen there, unaltered. Railroad cars and omnibusses run there constantly.

108. *Lowell Railroad.* — [See 88.]

109. *Fitchburg Railroad.* — [See 86.]

110. *Spring Hill*, in the town of Somerville.

111. *Prospect Hill, Waltham.* — A very extensive and varied view may be had from the top of this elevated ground. Waltham is eleven miles from Boston.

112. *Mount Auburn.* — Mount Auburn is a very beautiful rural cemetery, about four and a half miles distant. It was solemnly consecrated, with religious services, as a cemetery for the burial of the dead, September 24, 1831. The natural loveliness of the place is unsurpassable. It embraces about 110 acres of land — from the highest point of which, the eye is regaled with an extensive view of the most charming scenery. There are many good monuments and some statues there. The beautiful bronze statue of Bowditch, by Ball Hughes — the first bronze statue ever made in this country — may be seen there. It is of heroic size, and was placed there in 1847. Omnibusses and railroad cars from Boston pass there almost every hour.

113. *Harvard College, Cambridge.* — About four miles distant, and near Mount Auburn and Fresh Pond. [See Cambridge, 107.]

114. *McLean Insane Hospital* is in Somerville, on a beautiful spot once well known as "Barrell's Farm." It is an extensive building, well calculated for the purposes to which it is dedicated. Omnibusses pass it every hour.

115. *Grave-yard*, in Charlestown.

116. *Harvard's Monument.* — This monument bears the following inscription:

"HARVARD.

ON THE 16TH DAY OF SEPT. 1828,
THIS STONE WAS ERECTED
BY THE
GRADUATES OF THE UNIVERSITY OF CAMBRIDGE,
IN HONOR OF ITS FOUNDER,
WHO DIED AT CHARLESTOWN
ON THE
26TH DAY OF SEPT., A. D. 1638."

117. *Wachusett Mountain* is in Worcester county, and between 40 and 50 miles distant.

118. *Cambridge Observatory* belongs to the college, and is furnished with a large and very costly refracting telescope, imported from Munich, Germany, in 1847, at a cost of $20,000.

119. *Somerville* is a very pleasant and rapidly growing town, about three miles from Charlestown, and of which it was formerly a part. Is bounded north by Mystic River and Medford, west by West Cambridge, south by Cambridge, east by waters of the harbor and Charles River. It was set off by itself, under its present name, in 1842. Many houses are hid from view by the intervening hills. The cars of the Lowell, Maine, and Fitchburg roads pass through it. Population between 3 and 4000, and rapidly increasing.

120. *Cobble Hill.* — This hill is in Somerville, and is referred to in the histories of the revolution.

121. *Prospect Hill* was fortified at the commencement of the revolution; and this is one of the hills on which a portion of the American troops encamped at night, after the battle of Bunker Hill.

122. *Road to Cambridge.*

123. *Charlestown Neck.* — Now the boundary between Somerville and Charlestown.

124. *Causeway and Mill Dam.* — There is a saw-mill here, driven by the tide water.

125. *Monadnock Mountain*, in Jeffrey, N. H.; may be seen on a clear day.

126. *West Cambridge*, like most of the towns in the neighborhood, is filled with beautiful landscapes, and fine, cultivated grounds. It should be visited.

127. *Winter Hill.* — This hill was occupied by the Americans after the battle of Bunker Hill, and they entrenched themselves here on the night after the battle.

128. *Ruins of Ursuline Convent.* — This convent was destroyed by a mob in 1834.

129. *Mount Benedict.*

130. *Road to Medford.* — It was over this road that Stark led his brave troops to reinforce Col. Prescott, a few hours before the battle of Bunker Hill commenced.

131. *Canal.* — This canal, called the Middlesex Canal, was the first ever built in this country. It passes from the tide waters of Boston harbor to Lowell, 26 miles. It was 19 years in being built.

132. *Kearsarge Mountains*, at Newbury, N. H., may be seen when the atmosphere is very clear.

133. *White Mountains of N. H.* — The highest peak, Mount Washington, may be seen by a good-sighted person, when the atmosphere is very transparent.

134. *Medford* was settled in 1630. It is bounded on the south-west by Mystic River. Celebrated for ship building. Is a very pretty and flourishing town, containing much wealth and intelligence. Population about 5000. Distant about four miles. Cars pass there every hour in the day.

135. *Bunker Hill, Charlestown.* — By some writers Breed's Hill, on which the monument stands, is considered only a spur of Bunker Hill, — that is, that the *whole* of the elevated ground here is, properly, Bunker Hill.

136. *Stoneham.* — Incorporated 1725. Population nearly 2000. Celebrated for possessing a beautiful pond, of nearly 300 acres surface, affording choice sport to the angler. It is called Spot Pond. Distant about nine miles. Much frequented in summer. Easy of access by the railroad cars.

137. *Mystic River.* — The waters of Mystic River separate Somerville and Charlestown, from Medford, Malden, and Chelsea.

138. *Maine Railroad.* — [See 87.]

139. *Malden Bridge.* — This bridge is 2420 feet long, and, passing over Mystic River, unites Malden with Charlestown.

140. *Malden River.* — A small stream about six miles long, fed principally from Spot Pond, in Stoneham.

141. *Swan's Island.*

142. *Grave-yard*, in Charlestown.

143. *Malden*, formerly part of Charlestown. Set off in 1649. Distant about four and a half miles. Population between 3 and 4000. Omnibusses run there three or four times a day; and the cars of the Maine Railroad stop there half a dozen times a day. Melrose, in Malden, is a very pretty and favorite place.

144. *Saugus* is about nine miles from Boston. Formerly part of Lynn. Lynn was set off from Saugus in 1815. Eastern Railroad cars stop there repeatedly during the day.

145. *Island End River.* — This river, or bay, forms a part of the boundary between Chelsea and Malden.

146. *Lynn* is nine miles from Boston. Set off from Saugus in 1815. Population about 12,000. A thriving, industrious place. Celebrated for making shoes. Eastern Railroad cars stop there almost every hour in the day. Philips' Beach, in Lynn, is a charming place, and a favorite retreat during summer.

147. *U. S. Naval Hospital.* — This hospital is owned and supported by the United States, for the accommodation of seamen of the navy. Its situation is healthy and pleasant, and but a short distance from Chelsea Bridge. The attending physician's house is near the hospital, on the left.

148. *Cape Ann* is opposite Cape Cod, and the most northerly point of land in Massachusetts Bay.

149. *Marblehead* is a wild, romantic spot, peopled by a hardy and intrepid race of men. Is fourteen miles from Boston. Population about 6000. A branch of the Eastern Railroad passes through it, and cars stop frequently.

150. *Government Hill*, in Chelsea.

151. *Lynn Beach* is the most celebrated beach in the country, and is worth a visit. It is the neck of the peninsula of Nahant. Parties from the neighboring towns and cities visit it almost every day in summer.

152. *Chelsea*, formerly part of Boston, was set off in 1738. Indian name for it was "Winnisimmet." Chelsea beach is celebrated for its ocean roar in a storm, and is a fine place for a ride. The two United States hospitals are here. It is connected with Charlestown by a bridge, and with Boston by steam ferry boats. Is a very pleasant place, with a population of about 7000, and rapidly increasing.

153. *U. S. Marine Hospital.* — This hospital is distinct from the Naval Hospital, and is intended for sailors belonging to the merchant's service.

154. *Mount Bellingham.* — A beautiful rise of land, in Chelsea, commanding a good view of the harbor.

155. *Powder-horn Hill*, Chelsea.

156. *Chelsea Ferry Boat.* — [See 40.]

157. *Chelsea Bridge.* — This bridge is three fourths of a mile long, and crossing Mystic River, connects Chelsea with Charlestown.

158. *Nahant.* — Nahant has been a favorite summer retreat for many years. Steamboats run there every day in summer — Sundays *included* — and omnibusses, at Lynn, take passengers there from the Eastern Railroad cars. It is full of gayety and fashion, throughout the summer months.

159. *Little Nahant.* — Near Nahant, on Lynn Beach.

160. *Charlestown.* — Charlestown is the oldest town in Middlesex County. Was settled in 1628. Became a city in 1847. Population about 14,000. The Monument and the U. S. Navy Yard are here; and here was fought the battle of Bunker Hill — one of the bloodiest battles of the revolution.

THE BATTLE OF BUNKER HILL.

There is not an event in our history, perhaps, the particulars of which are more familiar to every one, than the "Battle of Bunker Hill" — yet it was thought that a very brief record of it should accompany this little work. The battle was fought on the 17th of June, 1775. In the evening of the day previous, the 16th of June, orders were given to Col. Prescott, with one thousand men, to occupy and defend Bunker Hill. The expedition was a secret one, and not unattended with danger, as the detachment were obliged to pass over Charlestown neck, which could at any moment be swept by the guns of three heavy batteries, floating near the shore — one of these the Glasgow sloop of war. The detachment left camp late in the evening, passed the neck in silence, and without alarming the English sentinels. Instead of proceeding to Bunker Hill, however, they marched to Breed's Hill — but whether this was done from mistake or from design, is not quite clear. The first account given of the battle by the Massachusetts Congress, (good authority, certainly,) says that Breed's Hill was fortified by mistake. By many, however, it is supposed that Breed's Hill was purposely selected, as the best and most advantageous position.* The fortifications were thrown up in about *four hours*, on the night, or morning rather, preceding the battle. The troops did not reach the summit of the hill until midnight, and at four o'clock in the morning the English batteries opened a hot fire on the American works. The entrenchments consisted of a redoubt and breastwork, made wholly of earth heaped by the spade. The redoubt was about eight rods square. Its southerly side, precisely parallel with the same

---

* During the day of the 17th, the Americans commenced entrenchments on Bunker Hill, and some little fighting took place there.

side of the present monument, was constructed with one projecting and two entering angles. The breastwork extended down the northern side of the hill about four hundred feet from, and in a line with, the eastern side of the redoubt, facing the present Navy Yard. There was a small space between the redoubt and breastwork, defended by a blind. The sally-port, entirely unprotected from within or without, opened on the northern side. It was undoubtedly the intention of the entrenchers to have run their breastwork down the entire side of the hill to the water, had time permitted — also to have protected their sally-port — but day dawned while they were in the midst of their labors, and with the dawn came the iron rain from the British batteries. Instead of being surprised that their works were not finished, we are amazed when we reflect how much they had accomplished in so short a time. Notwithstanding the incessant fire kept up by the enemies' batteries, the Americans continued to work at and strengthen their position during the morning. Boston was then the head-quarters of the English army; and as Breed's Hill overlooked Boston, it was at once determined by the English commander, to drive the Americans from their entrenchments. There were no bridges then between Boston and Charlestown, and communication between the two places was maintained by a ferry. About mid-day a detachment of two thousand troops, under Gen. Howe, came over from Boston, and landed, from barges, at Morton's Point, near the farthest point of the present Navy Yard. After landing, Gen. Howe considered his force too small for an attack, and sent for reinforcements, which soon arrived. While the English were awaiting the arrival of these additional troops, the Americans on the hill were reinforced by the arrival of about five hundred men from Cambridge and Medford, increasing their whole force to about fifteen hundred. While these events were passing, the neighboring eminences, church steeples, and roofs of houses, were crowded with anxious witnesses of the scene. The main body of the American army, encamped beyond Charlestown neck, were looking on, while Generals Burgoyne and Clinton, and many other English officers and citizens, observed all that passed from Copp's Hill. After being reinforced, Gen. Howe commenced ascending the hill. The Americans received the enemy's fire without returning it, and waited their approach, till they could "see the whites of their eyes," when they poured a stream of the most deadly and destructive fire upon the advancing columns; — rank after rank fell like grass before the mower's scythe, and the assailants were obliged to retreat. Though the enemy had suffered very severely, they rallied for another attack immediately on the arrival of more reinforcements from Boston, which were sent over to repair their losses. Again they advanced, and again were their close ranks thinned by the unerring shot of the Yankees in the redoubt and at the breastwork. Once more were the English put to flight and driven from the hill with terrible slaughter. During the second attack the town of Charlestown was purposely set on fire by bombs or rockets thrown from the Copp's Hill battery. It was during this attack, too, that the English overheard some of our men say that the ammunition was exhausted. After this second defeat of the English, Gen. Clinton came over from Boston with a fresh body of troops, again to reinforce Gen. Howe. The discovery made that the Americans were out of ammunition, made the regulars more willing to return a third time to the assault. The Americans again prepared to meet them; — the last few cartridges were distributed, and the very few men whose muskets were furnished with bayonets,* stood ready to use them, while many who had neither bayonets, nor powder, nor ball, determined to *make clubs of their guns*, and use them as they best could. A third time the English advanced. The fire from the American works was deadly at first, but soon slackened — and instead of bullets, the English found themselves assailed only with stones. They then felt that the strife was over — that they were contending with unarmed men. The Americans made a good and orderly retreat, and encamped at night on Winter and Prospect Hills, in Charlestown. The English manifested no disposition to pursue them, but entrenched themselves more securely on the heights they had so dearly purchased.

The number of English troops engaged in the fight on the hill could not have been less than four thousand. The whole number of the Americans did not exceed eighteen hundred.

The Americans were commanded by Col. Prescott — the English by Gen. Howe. The English loss was 1054, including 89 officers — viz.: 226 killed, 828 wounded. Total, 1054. The American loss was 115 killed and missing, 305 wounded, 30 taken prisoners. Total, 450. Besides the English force engaged in the fight on the hill, they had

A battery at Copp's Hill of 6 heavy guns and a mortar.

The Glasgow, sloop of war, of 24 guns and 175 men, lying near present Lowell Railroad.
" Somerset, ship of the line, " 70 " " 600 " " " Charlestown Bridge.
" Cerberus, frigate, " 36 " " 300 " " " off the present Navy Yard.
" Lively, corvette, " 28 " " 200 " " " Charlestown Bridge.
" Falcon, sloop of war " 20 " " 150 " " " off the present Navy Yard,

and two other vessels moored near to, and commanding Charlestown neck. All these heavy batteries kept up a more or less constant fire throughout the action, and, indeed, from the earliest morning dawn.

*Col Swett, in his account of the battle says, that there was "scarcely a bayonet to a company" — the guns were fowling-pieces of different calibres, and each man had to hammer or cut his bullets to fit his own gun. Most of the men had their powder in powder-horns, and some carried theirs in their pockets — very few of the men had cartridge-boxes.

THE MONUMENT.

BUNKER HILL MONUMENT stands in the centre of the ground that was enclosed by the walls of the old redoubt — its sides precisely parallel with those old walls. In 1824 an association, called the "Bunker Hill Monument Association," was formed, for the purpose of erecting a monument on this memorable spot. The corner-stone was laid by General Lafayette, on the 17th of June, 1825 — it being the fiftieth anniversary of the battle. There was a vast assemblage present on the occasion, including many patriotic soldiers of the Revolution. An eloquent address was delivered by the Hon. Daniel Webster.

The building of the monument was not actually commenced till 1827, when, after relaying the corner-stone, it was carried up a short distance, and then discontinued for the want of funds. It was finally completed in the summer of 1842 — the last stone being placed on the top, at six o'clock in the morning, on the 23d day of July, 1842.

It is built of Quincy granite, and the accompanying engraving of a section of the monument will convey a correct idea of its construction. The foundation is composed of six courses of stone, and extends twelve feet below the surface of the ground and base of the shaft. The four sides of the foundation extend about fifty feet horizontally. There are ninety courses of stone in the whole pile, six of them below the surface of the ground, and eighty-four above. The bottom, or base, of the monument is thirty feet square — at the top, or where the form of the apex begins, it is about fifteen feet square. The distance from the bottom to the top is two hundred and twenty-one feet. The stones themselves, measuring two hundred and nineteen feet and ten inches, and the mortar, in the seams between the stones, making up the balance of two hundred and twenty-one feet. Inside the shaft is a round hollow cone, the outside diameter of which, at the bottom, is ten feet, and on the inside, at the bottom, seven feet. At the top of the cone its outside diameter is six feet three inches, inside, four feet two inches. The observatory, or chamber, at the top of the monument, is seventeen feet in height and eleven feet in diameter. It has four windows — one on each side. Each window two

SECTION OF THE MONUMENT.

feet eight inches high and two feet two inches broad, provided with iron shutters. The walls at the door-way or entrance of the monument are six feet thick. The ascent to the top is made by a flight of two hundred and ninety-five steps. There are numerous little apertures in the cone and shaft for the purposes of ventilation and light. The cap-piece, or apex, of the monument, is a single stone, three feet six inches in thickness, and four feet square at its base — weighing two and a half tons. The height of each of the five courses of stone composing the point of the monument, is twenty inches — all the other courses, seventy-eight in number, are two feet eight inches in height.

The monument was designed by Mr. Solomon Willard, of Boston, architect, and built by Mr. James Savage, of Boston.

In 1794, King Solomon's Lodge of Freemasons erected a monument to the memory of Warren and his associates, who fell in the battle of Bunker Hill. This monument stood outside of the redoubt, on the spot where Gen. Warren was supposed to have fallen. It was a handsome structure, composed of a very graceful Tuscan pillar, about twenty feet high, standing on a pedestal ten or twelve feet high, and surmounted by a golden urn, bearing the inscription, "J. W., aged 35," entwined with masonic emblems. The south side of the pedestal bore the following inscription: —

ERECTED A. D. 1794,
BY
KING SOLOMON'S LODGE
OF
FREEMASONS,
(CONSTITUTED IN CHARLESTOWN, 1783,)
IN MEMORY OF
MAJOR GENERAL JOSEPH WARREN,
AND HIS ASSOCIATES,
WHO WERE SLAIN ON THIS MEMORABLE SPOT,
JUNE 17, 1775.

"None but those who set a just value upon the blessings of
Liberty are worthy to enjoy her.

"In vain we toiled; in vain we fought; — we
bled in vain, if you, our offspring, want
valor to repel the assaults
of her invaders."

When the present monument was completed, the Masonic Lodge placed a beautiful model of the old monument inside of the new one. This model stands directly in front of the entrance.

Printed by Libri Plureos GmbH in Hamburg, Germany